I'm Roger Federer, and I'm on top
when it comes to the tennis court.
Tennis is much more than hitting a ball.
You have to be fast, skilled, and even
witty to win the game.

To many, I'm one of the all-time greats.
But I was born without any skills.
I had to teach myself.

I was born in Switzerland,
and from the point when I learned
how to walk, I loved sports!

I played basketball and badminton.
Badminton is kind of like tennis, but
we hit this feathery thing called a shuttlecock.

Playing sports at a young age
helped me grow my hand-eye coordination.
That's when your hands move fast to
whatever your eyes see. You need to have that
if you want to play tennis!

I kept playing, and I loved watching others play as well. I watched other famous tennis players and learned a lot from them.

I soon grew big enough to play
in the junior teams. In 1998,
I led my team to victory. By the end
of the year, I was number one for my age!
The century was turning, and so was my life.

I kept playing, eventually winning
my first ever Master Series in 2002,
one of the biggest tennis tournaments.

However, I didn't win every game.
One thing people believe about us
superstars is that we can never lose.

But I became a tennis superstar because
I've lost many times. In my first tournament
as a professional, I even lost in the first round.

Just like you, I have my losses. Sometimes, I'm just having a bad day. Other times, my opponent is even stronger than I am.

But I don't let the losses get me down.
Every time I lost, I learned from it and
wondered how I could improve for the next game.

In 2003, I won my first Grand Slam
title at Wimbledon.

I watched how my rival played, and I would try to figure out how I can beat him.

And because of this, I grew stronger.
I won more singles titles than I could count,
breaking so many records it was hard
to believe. I soon rose to the top.

And yet, I knew there were those who were suffering. I used my stardom to help out those who were poor. I gave my money to charities, and even helped those who were suffering because of hurricanes and earthquakes.

I believe if life gives you fortune,
you should help spread it to those who
may not be able to play tennis or
achieve their dreams.

I'm 35 now, an age where many players are winding down and ready to retire. But I'm still playing! I even won my fifth Australia Open in 2017 after hurting myself and having to take a little break.

Get more inspirational children books by Roy Brandon!

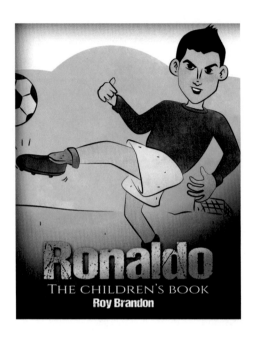

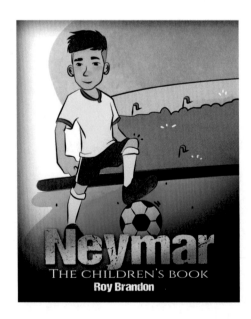

Visit www.RoyBrandon.com for more...

Made in the USA
Middletown, DE
20 April 2019